e
04/02/05
310

Marie's Journey

Marie's Journey

A True Account of
Overcoming Child Abuse

By Yvonne Rimmer

Marie's Journey

by Yvonne Rimmer

© 1998, Word Aflame Press
   Hazelwood, MO 63042-2299

Cover Design by Paul Povolni

All Scripture quotations in this book are from the King James Version of the Bible unless otherwise identified.

This story is true, but the names have been changed to protect the privacy of the people involved.

Printed in United States of America

Printed by

WORD AFLAME®PRESS
8855 DUNN ROAD
HAZELWOOD, MO 63042-2299

Library of Congress Cataloging-in-Publication Data

Rimmer, Yvonne
   Marie's Journey / Yvonne Rimmer.

         ISBN 1-56722-224-2
         Data applied for

$\mathcal{D}$edication ✍

First, I dedicate this book to the Lord of my life, Jesus Christ, who gave me the strength and inspiration to write this book. May He always be first in my life!

Second, to my husband, Timothy, for his love, support, and strength during my journey of healing and our life together and for encouraging the publication of this book.

Third, to Dennis Anderson for his prayers and support as my pastor and to his wife, Susan Anderson, for her strength and love as a friend and pastor's wife to encourage healing in my life and the publication of this book.

Fourth, to Jan Donham, a friend who heard the call of God to help the abused and reached out a helping hand.

And, finally, for the reason of this book: to the abused and those who will stand in the gap to help those who are hurting. May the Lord direct us all!

Contents

Foreword

Knowing what I know about hurting people, I find myself watching little children everywhere I go, wondering what private nightmare they might be involved in. I am so thrilled that Yvonne Rimmer ventured to write this book! She possesses a rare courage that so many of us lack today. It is the courage of Esther, who had come to the kingdom for "such a time as this." The result of this kind of courage is that God can use such a person! Jesus Christ is the Answer. He is always the Answer. But Jesus uses people. Our hands, our words, our feet, our arms can help bring healing to those He sends our way.

I know that it is Yvonne Rimmer's prayer and desire to be used by God. And it is my prayer and desire that, after reading *Marie's Journey*, you will take the time to reach out and to love every child you meet . . . and every adult who might have a secret, hurting child living inside.

Lynda Allison Doty, Ph.D.

The pain in her eyes and the words from her lips told a story I was not prepared to hear. The young lady kept asking if I was sure I could handle this. I knew I could not handle it by myself, but God would give me the strength to help bear her burden by just listening and offering what encouragement I could.

She began to speak of hurt, pain, and suffering. Her words came slowly—sometimes even haltingly. There was embarrassment, anger, and frustration—a deep well of emotions. There were physical and mental scars, even questions about her own integrity. How could a mere child attract such negative attention from a grown man?

Why did she have to miss a normal childhood and experience more tumultuous than normal teenage years? Why was she suffering even now as a young married lady with children?

There are far too many stories very closely related to this one. While we do not understand what goes on in the minds of people who commit these atrocities, we know a God who can heal both the victim and the perpetrator. Thank You, Lord, for loving us unconditionally and restoring so many who have been physically and emotionally abused.

And thank you, Yvonne, for sharing the story of Marie, who learned to give her situation to God, remembering daily, "For God hath not given us the spirit of fear; but of power, and of love, and of a sound mind" (II Timothy 1:7).

May God use this story to show those who are hurting that there is hope and healing in Him, and may they experience His genuine, unfailing love.

Susan Anderson
Pastor's wife
Apostolic Faith Tabernacle
Pearcy, Arkansas

Preface

Abuse is not only hard to admit but is extremely delicate to deal with in today's world. As I have listened to many testimonies and talked with many women, I have found that abuse is more prevalent today than ever. There must be those who will hear the call of God and reach for those who are hurting!

In dealing with abuse from my own past I felt the Lord began to stir my heart to reach to those who are hurting. Because, all too well, I understand and know the pain from an abused life. I know the guilt, the embarrassment, the shame, the pain, and the search for the love that was stripped away as a child. As God spoke and inspired, I began to write and this book came forth. It is dedicated to the glory of God to see many healed and delivered and for a ministry that is greatly needed!

One 🐛

Awakened!

s she suddenly awakened in the midst of the night, she felt an eerie presence.

Marie cried out for an answer, but there was none. Her heart pounded rapidly in her chest as she struggled for the bedside lamp. Instantly the light pierced the darkness, but there was no one except her husband sleeping peacefully beside her. As she reached to turn off the light, she felt the presence lurking in the shadows.

Settling back into her bed, she began to pray for God to overshadow the room with His peace.

The next morning came as early as they

all had. Marie struggled to get up from the bed, feeling extremely tired. She went into her sons' bedroom, noticing how peaceful they looked. Remembering the night before, she shook it off as a bad dream.

She got the same response as the other mornings when she reached to wake up her two sons. "Just a few more minutes," they pleaded as they reluctantly crawled from their beds. Turning to leave the room, she reminded them to hurry so they could pray before catching the bus.

Entering the room of her older daughter she heard the same argument as with the boys. Before she could answer, the baby began to cry from her room. Rushing to prepare a bottle before the baby woke up Dad, Marie urged her daughter to get dressed.

After settling the baby, she hurried back to check on the progress of the other children and found her older son on the floor sound asleep. While Marie struggled to pull him from the floor, he pleaded with her that he had gotten out of bed. "Now let's try getting dressed,"

Marie answered as the other children chuckled.

Glancing at her other children in hopes of settling them before an argument started, she fought the urge to laugh. Her younger son had definitely dressed himself. His hair looked as if it was in the army, standing at attention. His shirt was inside out, and his socks had lost their partner. Marie, trying to obtain a straight face, asked who had helped him get dressed. Of course, she knew the answer: he had done it all on his own.

With a proud look, her younger son, Tyler, asked, "How do I look?"

Marie tried to answer as best she could without laughing. But finally she replied, "If you're ever going to get married, there are a few things you need to learn."

Tyler quickly announced, "That's okay, I don't need to learn anything. I'm never leaving home."

Trying to dress him again, Marie quickly changed the subject, pleading with her children to hurry so they wouldn't miss the bus. Ready to go, they stumbled behind her, swinging backpacks and coats everywhere. Marie gathered her children into the living room for prayer. When they had begun, Marie fell to her knees beside them.

Something deep within stirred as she heard her children's prayers. She prayed for their safety and for God's direction in their lives. She cried aloud as she pleaded for the blood of Jesus to cover each child. Still there was something she couldn't explain, a feeling that troubled her soul.

Continuing to pray that God would take away the disquieting feeling, she heard the excitement of the children next door. She realized that the school bus was rounding the corner down the road. Ending their prayer, each child gave her the usual kiss and hug before they stampeded out the door toward the bus stop. Marie sighed a deep breath of relief, knowing they were safely on their way.

So began Marie's day. After a few minutes of rest, it was time to see her husband off to work, to take care of the baby, and to begin the laundry. As the day unfolded, she received a call from a distraught friend, who faced a family tragedy, and a visit from her father-in-law, who informed her that her husband's uncle was dying of cancer.

Then it was time to hurry to church for volunteer work and on to the grocery store. After returning home, Marie put the baby down for a nap and took some time to pray and read the Bible. She received another call from her friend to say that the family crisis was resolved. Marie rejoiced with her.

Before long, the children were home from school, and it was time to help with homework and prepare dinner. Her husband came home, and the family had dinner. Afterwards, the children began to take their baths and get ready for bed.

After their prayers, Marie hurried each child to bed and tucked them in. Then she finished the chores of the day and collapsed in her chair. Relaxing, she recalled the day's events and thanked the Lord for such a perfect life. Except for the everyday hassles, Marie was completely settled with her life. She was blessed with good children and a wonderful and caring husband. Marie and her family were greatly blessed by God. Even though they didn't have many material possessions, they had God and each other. The love that God had given them was all that mattered.

Two 🌿

Struggling to Understand

A few nights later, Marie lay paralyzed in her bed as the dark presence once again returned. As she struggled to move, she realized her body was lifeless. She gasped for another breath and attempted to scream, but she heard only the silence of the night. Her heart pounded as she watched the dark image disappear into the night. She shook under the cover, and sweat beaded across her forehead.

Finally Marie sprang from her bed and began to search the house diligently. The children were sleeping peacefully. With her heart still pounding from fear, Marie prayed for peace to settle in her heart as she slid under the covers.

The image kept returning night after night. Marie soon realized it was only going to get worse. During an afternoon of prayer, Marie felt led to anoint her bed and the door posts throughout the house. She felt the presence of the Lord enter the room.

That night, Marie was completely at peace. She fell asleep only to be awakened by an eerie voice calling her name. The image had reappeared. She cried out for an answer, but none came. She closed her eyes tightly and rebuked the voice and image in Jesus' name. She lunged at the image and heard it call her name again. Marie fell to the floor with a loud crash and began to weep. Staggering into her living room she knelt down to pray, hoping to find understanding. Finally she felt a release in her spirit, returned to bed, and soon drifted off to sleep.

As the nights went on, the tormenting images became terrorizing dreams. Sometimes, Marie, trying to attack the images in her dreams, would find herself attacking her husband. Her loud screams would wake him, and he would comfort her. Marie prayed that the dreams would get better, but they became worse. Soon they began to affect her daily routine.

Marie's thirst for God grew deeper. She became desperate to draw closer to God. Marie was determined not to backslide, as she loved the truth too much. The old life had nothing to offer; it had lost its appeal. As each church service came and went, however, Marie's desperation began to grow deeper. As she struggled to find answers, she grew downhearted and slowly began to lose hope. She continued to search for understanding at each turn. What had happened to her peaceful life? Had she done something to turn God away? Where was God, and why wouldn't He answer her?

One night, Marie and her husband found out that time was short for her husband's uncle. The family gathered at his bedside as death approached. On entering the house where he lay, Marie felt a dark presence. She touched the dying man and watched as life drained from him. Soon his body was cold and lifeless. To Marie he seemed like a frozen rock, and to her surprise, she realized that on the inside she felt the same way herself.

What had brought her life crashing down? she wondered. She hadn't felt this way in years.

The dreams continued, and as they did, eventually things started becoming clearer. It was as if Marie could see her life reflected in a mirror; her tormenting past had come back to destroy her.

Marie began remembering her childhood. Tears filled her eyes, and fear gripped her heart. The physical and mental abuse she suffered from a stepfather and others began to haunt her again. Her childhood horrors began to flood her every thought.

As a child she had become hardened in trying to cope with the abuse she had suffered. No matter the severity of the abuse, Marie had learned to hide her fears within the walls she had erected around her. She would not allow anyone ever to hurt her again. Anger built up within her, the walls around her grew stronger, and she grew callused to those around her. No one seemed to sense her pain. Feeling abandoned by everyone, Marie withdrew into herself as the flames of her suffering engulfed her.

Marie closed her eyes as tightly as she could, trying to avoid the images now racing through her mind. Somehow hoping to escape the hideous thoughts, she wandered outside. As she strove to regain her composure, she fell against a tree, and burning tears streamed down her cheeks.

She felt the belt as it hit her over and over again. The pain slashed through her again and again as the belt began to burn into her body. One blow would drive her out, as the next awakened her. Stumbling to her feet Marie cried aloud to God, as she gazed toward heaven, "I was only a child. Why did it happen to me?" Laughter, friends, and family were forgotten as her childhood had been stripped away from her.

Then the horrible visions of the sexual abuse began. Marie tried to fight them off as the terrorizing thoughts took control of her mind. She was an innocent child, with great expectations still in her life. But they were all altered one night as Marie was awakened by a noise. Not realizing the evil forces that had intruded into her room, Marie called out for an answer. There in the shadows stood her stepfather, watching her. Marie noticed the stench of alcohol as he drew closer. The smile upon his face became firm as he reached for her. Even now she felt his every touch as he captured her.

As he began to abuse her, she cried silently from within, and confusion took control of her. She struggled to get away, but she felt his breath, his grip tightened, and pain ravaged her body. He finally became weary. Marie heard his laughter as his grip loosened. She slowly eased back towards the wall in hopes of escape as he reached to grasp her throat. "If you ever tell anyone I'll . . . I'll . . . !" he threatened as he stumbled from her room. When he left, Marie began picking up the pieces of her childhood that his violent act had so brutally shattered.

Trying to escape this nightmare, Marie quickly slid out her bedroom window and staggered frantically into the woods. She crawled into an underground culvert and turned quickly to confirm that she wasn't being followed. As she lay cradled like a baby, Marie sought desperately to make some sense out of what had happened. She searched for answers. Why was he so angry? What had she done that was so terrible as to deserve a punishment as severe as this?

Whatever she had done wrong, she had to prevent herself from doing it in the future. This punishment was the most severe she had ever experienced, and pain continued to surge through her body. Longing for someone to ease the pain, Marie cried uncontrollably and eventually drifted off to sleep.

Each time the abuse seemed to get worse. Marie's stepfather took every opportunity he had. He began to thrive on the impossible. He loved to be daring and catch Marie when she least expected it. Even when the family would gather together he took his chances. No one else knew what was happening, but Marie began to anticipate his every move.

Each time the abuse would destroy a piece of Marie, until she felt worthless and demoralized. No matter how far she would run, he would always find her. No matter how hard she tried to forget, the thoughts were always there.

Trying to salvage what little dignity she had, Marie began to search for peace at school. She tried to be tough, and as a result Marie found herself getting into a lot of fights. Pulling Marie off another student, her teacher, Mrs. Baker, asked, "What is wrong with you? Last year you were so easygoing, and you were so tender. Why have you become so harsh?"

Dusting herself off, Marie argued, "She started it!"

"It doesn't matter who started it; you both know better," replied Mrs. Baker. "Dawn, you go that direction, and Marie, you go to my office now!" Mrs. Baker ordered as she pointed towards the door.

Walking into the office, Mrs. Baker motioned for Marie to take a seat as she shut the door behind her. "Now!" Mrs. Baker questioned, "Do you mind telling me what is going on inside your head? I have never seen you lose control like that before. And I want the truth!" Mrs. Baker demanded as she gazed at Marie.

Marie, still aggravated from the fight, snapped, "Do you really care?"

"Yes, as a matter of fact I do care!" replied Mrs. Baker as she fought back the tears. "Something has really disturbed you, and I want to help. But you must understand, my duty as a teacher requires me to inform the right authorities if you tell me certain things."

Dropping her head, Marie knew she couldn't say anything. The threats of her abuser rang through her mind as she held back her tears. "I'm fine," Marie choked as she turned to leave.

As she opened the door, Marie felt a hand on her shoulder. "Remember, if you ever want to talk, I'm here anytime," Mrs. Baker softly answered.

Not able to face Mrs. Baker, Marie nodded

her head as she left the office. Marie soon became good friends with Mrs. Baker but never allowed her inner secrets to be discovered. Sometimes Marie wanted to trust her and ask for help, but the ugliness she would uncover was too much to deal with. She didn't want anyone to see the secrets she had buried inside. Guilt had overwhelmed Marie until she believed that no one could ever understand what she was going through. Feeling that she was wrong for allowing the abuse to happen, she blamed herself for everything. She believed she would lose her teacher's friendship if she ever trusted her with the secret, or worse yet, the threats of her abuser would be fulfilled. So Marie held her silence.

Three

A Narrow Escape

Marie's stringy hair fell into her eyes as she followed along closely behind her brothers. She was covered with sweat and dirt, but she cherished the times they played together, for it was the joy of her life. She would image herself as a great explorer, and her brothers would use her to experiment with new adventures. Swinging from vines, tubing down snow-covered hills, and burrowing through undiscovered tunnels, Marie was completely confident of herself. Even though most of the time she would end up hurt and they would often end up carrying her home, Marie never minded as long as she was allowed to participate. As a child from a divorced family, Marie held on to the other children, feeling that they were all she had. She had a fear that she would lose them as she had lost her father.

But soon the abuse began to silence the child inside Marie. She withdrew into herself. She found it impossible to trust anyone, and the pain of the abuse began to destroy even her relationships with her family.

Marie began sneaking off for hours to escape into her own little world. Soon her youthful life fled as the days passed by. She kept her sanity by dreaming of the life that she would live when she could leave home.

When she returned home one night from a school function, Marie found her mother stricken with terror because of her stepfather. Seeing her tear-stained face, Marie knew she could stand no more. A demonic spirit captivated Marie's thoughts. She vowed to seek revenge on the one who had destroyed her life. She reached for a bat and set out to accomplish her mission.

Bursting through the door of her stepfather's trailer, Marie began breaking every-thing in her path. She wanted desperately to destroy the life that had so easily destroyed hers. As she beat her stepfather repeatedly, Marie felt an unseen hand reach down to stop her from killing her abuser. Terrified by her thoughts, Marie quickly dropped the bat and ran frantically from the trailer.

She ran until exhaustion took control. Her knees buckled, and tears of pain burned down her cheeks. Even though he had hurt her, she knew she didn't want to be like him. She began to realize that her life would never be the same. There was no turning back.

As the days passed, Marie encountered many hardships in her struggle to survive on her own. There were many sleepless nights without a roof over her head or even a morsel of food to eat. She searched for peace, drifting from town to town. Hoping desperately to outrun the horrifying thoughts of her past, she only encountered them again in the next town.

Marie longed for peace in her heart, but

as the years passed she found herself becoming hardened. Each day the hate she had toward herself would increase. She became cold and bitter on the outside but cried painfully from within. She longed to reach out for help, but knowing the pain she'd have to suffer, she kept her silence. Marie could help others in pain, but there was nothing she could do to help herself.

Marie discovered that the laughter she shared with friends could help her forget her troubles. She made many friends, but she never allowed them to intrude upon her inner feelings. She used laughter in an attempt to push away the abuse that had controlled her for so long.

Finally settling in an unfamiliar town, she became obsessed with job, college, and career. She left no time for rest or for life itself.

Soon, however, her life began deteriorating before her eyes. As the pressures of life overwhelmed her, Marie turned to alcohol and drugs. She especially sought the numbness that alcohol would bring. She convinced herself that it helped her sleep throughout the night. But within, the poison slowly destroyed the life that struggled to live.

Those around her began to notice something was wrong, and they pleaded with Marie to slow down. But she began to depend more upon drugs to ease her pain, as alcohol was no longer strong enough. She tried to use laughter to hide her pain, but she found it impossible to clear her mind. Pushing herself harder each day, Marie found exhaustion taking over. She depended upon drugs for strength, but she soon felt addicting urges taking control. Fighting the urges only caused Marie to explode with anger.

As Marie struggled to do her job her boss became extremely worried. Noticing that her hands were swollen and her eyes were bloodshot, she took Marie to her office. "Marie, you have got to get help," her boss pleaded. "You are going to kill yourself if you don't slow down."

"I'll be fine," Marie insisted as she collapsed to the floor.

With no energy to refuse help, Marie was rushed to the doctor's office. Realizing that she was having a stroke, the doctor rushed her to the hospital. All feeling in her left side had gone; her brain had shut it down. As Marie lay almost lifeless in the hospital she wondered, Why don't I just die? Why am I still alive? Her will to live was shattered.

A few days later a preacher entered her hospital room. He introduced himself and announced that God had sent him. "You can't outrun God," he told her. "He is always there!" As he prayed with her, Marie felt a heavenly presence enter the room, and she felt hope again.

Within a month, Marie had completely recovered and was ready to face the world. She felt rested and back on top as she left the hospital. She had beaten death once again.

As she gradually returned to her everyday life, she soon forgot the preacher God had sent.

As time went on, Marie began to get homesick. Desperately hoping to rekindle a burnt-out relationship with her family, Marie returned home. She struggled to restore what the abuse had shattered, but she soon realized that too much damage had been done. The wounds were just too great to heal.

One day her mother and sister announced that they were moving. Marie was devastated, for she couldn't leave with them. She had just received a job promotion and was finally becoming stable. Watching them leave, Marie knew all hopes of reuniting her family were gone.

Marie turned to her job to soothe her pain, and she again sought refuge in laughter. No one ever knew what to expect from her, but there was never a dull moment. She was always the one they turned to for fun. Marie loved the laughter because it made the pain diminish.

She did not realize it at the time, but she made an impact on more lives than she knew. The jokes, pranks, and fun drew the employees together as a family. She cherished those times, and they made the workday enjoyable.

Four

A Glorious Revelation

Soon Marie entered into a relationship with a man. He became abusive, and Marie soon found out that she was pregnant. It became harder to laugh. Her loneliness grew deeper.

She knew the baby was a gift from God, and she knew her child deserved a better life than what she had. Each day her love for her daughter grew stronger as she watched the tiny life cling to her. But the fear of destroying her child was overwhelming. How could she raise her alone, when she couldn't even help herself? Struggling with decisions, Marie knew she was not fit to be a mother. But her love for the child was so great that she couldn't bear to live without her.

One night Marie began to write her final good-byes. She searched for a pistol that she had hid in her dresser drawer. As she grasped the cold, deadly weapon in her hands, tears began to stream down her face. Horrifying thoughts of her abusive past once again began to torment her mind. What a failure I have been, she thought, and there is nothing to show for my life.

As she raised the weapon to her mouth, Marie froze with fear. She felt as if someone was watching. When she glanced around, no one was there, but the presence still lingered. Marie looked down at her weapon and became greatly disturbed.

Suddenly the preacher's words from a few years back began to ring through her mind. Dropping to her knees, Marie reminded God of His promise. "God, if You are always there, where are You now?" Marie cried out in distress. She continued to plead with God to help her.

Trembling with fear, she loosened her grip on the pistol, and it fell from her sweaty hands. Pushing it under the couch, she knew she had to occupy her mind, or the evil thoughts would win. She didn't want to die, but neither could she live with herself any longer. Marie pulled herself up from the floor, and she hurried to make herself busy.

Later that night, Marie was surprised by an unexpected knock at her door. To her shock, standing there was Dawn, the secretary from her job.

She had only spoken to Dawn a few times in passing at work. Marie realized that she didn't need to be alone, so she invited Dawn in and asked her to stay for dinner. Dawn gratefully accepted the invitation.

After dinner Marie began clearing the table, and Dawn began to ask why God had led her there. Realizing that God had heard her cry, Marie began to weep bitterly. Dawn reached out to help. Marie couldn't understand why she was trusting a total stranger but found it impossible to hold back her emotions. Pain flooded her mind, and tears of anguish burned down her cheeks.

What made Dawn so different? Marie wondered. Why was there such peace when she was around? She knew Dawn was a Christian, but she was like none Marie had ever known before. There was something unusual about her character. She had a glow that Marie didn't understand, and Marie felt a divine presence when she was near.

As Marie talked about her life, Dawn listened with a concern and love like no other. As the night pressed on, the two became friends, crying and laughing together.

They also read the Word of God together. Marie tried to present her own beliefs but was never able to base her opinion on the Bible. The Lord began to impress many verses upon Dawn as she witnessed to Marie throughout the night.

When the morning light began to peer through the window, Marie knew it was time for Dawn to return home. Watching her leave, Marie felt sad but more secure.

Marie's curiosity about what Dawn had told her began to overwhelm her. She decided to go to the library to do research on her own. Searching book after book, Marie shook her head in disbelief. She read how many religions were formed by humans, but the apostolic doctrine that Dawn had presented had a biblical foundation. Never had Marie studied the Bible on her own; she had just accepted the words of others until now. Her thirst grew as the books piled upon the table. Losing all sense of time, Marie studied throughout the day until the library closed.

The next time Dawn came by, Marie was overflowing with new questions. Marie wanted biblical answers. As the two studied, Marie's anticipation grew. She yearned to know more about the apostolic doctrine.

From time to time Dawn even brought over a few friends from her church, and soon they too became Marie's friends. Marie watched the life they lived and found herself longing to be like them. There was a mystery about them. They had an inner peace and happiness that Marie had searched for all her life. So when they invited her to go to church, Marie was eager to go.

Marie felt the hair on the back of her neck stand up as she entered the church. The evil spirits that resided in her soul caused her body to shake nervously. She felt the dark spirits inside as they battled to maintain control. Struggling to sit down, Marie quickly slid onto the pew beside Dawn.

The church service was like none she had ever experienced. The exuberant worship and singing was exciting as the voices filled the room. Each face had the same joy and glow that Marie had noticed on Dawn's face. As the preacher began to speak, Marie soaked up the words. The more she heard, the more she began to feel conviction of sin. When the altar call came, she dropped her head, and her fingers gripped the pew. Feeling shame from her past, Marie slowly eased back down into her pew.

On the drive home, anger flooded Marie's mind. The tears streaming down her face notified Dawn that something was wrong. She tried to show compassion to help ease Marie's fears but realized the best answer was to pray.

Dawn invited Marie back to church, but Marie reluctantly denied her offer as she closed the car door behind her. Entering her apartment, Marie felt loneliness. The spirit of depression once again took control.

Not a day passed without Marie's thinking about the church and her newfound friends. But no one could do anything to brighten her day. She found herself watching Dawn at work. She seemed to have what Marie was searching for. Dawn always had an encouraging word and was always there to offer a smile to brighten her day.

One day Dawn invited Marie to dinner and a day of shopping. Marie hadn't been out in a long time and figured it would do her some good. The day brought fun and laughter as the two scurried about the town. Marie felt as if she had hurt Dawn by refusing her offer to return to church but was grateful that she was so understanding.

On the way home Marie realized that they

were heading a different way. "Why are we going this direction?" Marie asked.

"I want you to meet my family," Dawn replied.

"No, Dawn! I can't meet them now!" Marie pleaded as she began to shake nervously.

"Why not?" Dawn questioned with a bewildered look.

"I don't look good enough," Marie answered nervously, trying to hide the actual reason.

"You'll love them!" pleaded Dawn, in hopes of encouraging Marie.

"No, I'm not going!" Marie argued as they pulled into the driveway.

"Too late; we are already here," Dawn announced as she stepped from the car. Despite all the refusals from Marie, Dawn would not take no for an answer. Insisting that everything would be fine, she persuaded Marie into the house and introduced her to the family.

Laughter filled the air, bringing back something Marie hadn't felt in ages. This family was full of love and excitement. Dawn's mother made her feel right at home with her teasing and openness. Love and tenderness flowed from her every word.

Marie froze with fear as she heard Dawn announce, "Dad is here!" Marie tried desperately to smile as he entered the room. Shaking his hand, Marie noticed the tender appearance that seemed to beam from his glowing countenance.

Dawn's family had compassion and love for people like no one else she had met. The atmosphere was so different from what Marie had expected. It wasn't full of fighting and bad feelings. Marie even found herself relaxing within the comfort of Dawn's family.

But the hours passed, and eventually Marie had to return home to her empty apartment. She longed even more to know what Dawn and her family had.

The next time Marie saw Dawn, Dawn invited her to return to church again. Marie went, and this time she felt a little more secure.

With each visit, Marie felt more comfortable. She even began to draw closer to some of the families within the church. Her desire to draw closer to Jesus grew stronger each day. She didn't understand it completely, but she wasn't going to give up until she found out more about the wonderful experience she had read about in her Bible.

One night during a revival meeting, Marie listened closely to the evangelist. He talked about a promise that she too could have. Thirsting for truth, Marie pondered every word carefully.

Tears fell from her face. She knew she was unworthy, but she stepped into the aisle. Feeling the tug of the Spirit, Marie pressed forward and knelt at an altar. "Lord Jesus," she prayed, "please forgive me for all the wrong in my life. I know I've done a lot of unjust things, but I really want to change. I need Your help and guidance. Lord, without You I can't . . . I won't live without You. Without You I am nothing. Please, Lord, help me."

Pouring her burdens out to God, she felt the hands of those around her, and she felt a divine presence. She heard the effective, fervent prayers of those around her as they ascended to God. Not knowing how to continue, Marie embraced the altar harder. She was determined not to quit until she received what she so earnestly sought. As Marie cried out in the name of Jesus, something began to happen. A strong presence overshadowed her, and peace began to touch her soul. Crying aloud to the Lord, she continued repenting and asking for forgiveness.

In the past she had run from God and had blamed Him for all her difficulties. She realized that she continued to live in turmoil and pain because of her own decisions. Marie began to express bitter remorse for her life before God and to cry for His grace and mercy. She knew that she was unworthy, but she had heard the preacher say God was willing to give salvation to "whosoever will." Marie pleaded with God that she couldn't go on without Him and didn't even want to try. She diligently besought God to let her die if He couldn't save her, because she knew that without God all hope was lost and her life was nothing.

She stood to her feet and raised her hands

into the air. As worship poured from her lips, she felt her burdens lifting. Trembling all over, she humbly bowed to her knees and began speaking in other tongues. A heavenly presence overshadowed her as the glorious Holy Ghost fell upon her. Marie became lost in her experience with the Lord. She was enveloped in the arms of Jesus.

Marie's countenance began to glow when she realized that this was the same experience she had read about in her Bible. Joy and peace filled her heart. Marie knew instantly that her prayers had been answered and her life would never be the same as she rejoiced in the goodness of the Lord. Now God was not only with her, but He was in her. The angelic host rejoiced with the church as another lost sinner returned home.

The next weekend Marie rejoiced again as she was lifted from the baptismal waters in Jesus' name. Her salvation was complete. She was ready to live her life for the One who had so mercifully saved her!

Five

True Forgiveness

*M*arie's coworkers soon noticed the change in her life. She was eager to tell them of the biblical truth that God had revealed to her but was surprised to find out that many didn't accept it. Ignoring the conversations around her, Marie continued to grow in her experience.

As Marie began to grow in the Lord she felt an unsettling feeling that something wasn't right. She questioned Dawn about it and soon got an answer that she didn't want to accept. Shaking her head in disbelief, she felt anger begin to surface from the past.

Since she had received the Holy Ghost,

Marie had avoided those who had abused her. Now Dawn told her that she needed to learn to forgive them and to seek forgiveness for wrong things she had done. Dawn explained that if she wanted forgiveness she too had to forgive. Jesus said in Matthew 6:14, "For if ye forgive men their trespasses, your heavenly Father will also forgive you. But if ye forgive not men their trespasses, neither will your father forgive your trespasses."

Marie felt betrayed by Dawn. Why should she be the one to offer forgiveness and ask for forgiveness? Nevertheless, she dedicated herself to prayer and fasting about the matter.

Marie finally began to see the person inside of her. The darkened images that began to surface were full of tremendous hatred and pain. The ugliness began to reveal itself as she fought to hide it. Contending with the truth that Dawn had spoken, Marie began to weep. She knew the time had come to face those who had destroyed her childhood innocence. She had to release the anger that had been bottled up for so many years, before it devastated her life.

Struggling with the decision that she knew was right, she prayed for strength and direction.

A few weeks later Marie was compelled to call one of her abusers. Summoning all the courage she could, she choked on her words as she clenched the receiver. She tried to hold back her tears as anger rose within, but she offered forgiveness.

Her abuser merely responded with lies, blaming alcohol and drugs in an attempt to evade guilt. Marie knew that she had journeyed to a dead end. She sadly hung up the phone. Grasping her knees, she fell to the floor. Her childhood memories became so real as she sat there weeping alone. She felt completely life-less, but she knew she had done what was right.

Trying to pray, she could only weep. But as the tears burned, she felt thc hatred began to fade away. To ease the anguish and gain control of herself, Marie began to wipe the tears from her eyes. Soon realizing that she needed God's help, she began to cry out loud to the Lord.

Instantly, Marie felt a heavenly presence overshadow her as the arms of the Lord wrapped around her and He began to minister to her. She knew then that she did not have to suffer any longer because Jesus was there to help her.

Six

The Promise of Happiness

As Marie's journey continued with God, she failed Him many times, but she realized that He would never leave her. The devil and his forces fought her at every turn, but she was determined to hold on. She felt so unworthy at times but knew God's grace was for people like her. She didn't have much to offer, but she was willing to give it all to Him. She didn't always understand the trials and hardships that came her way, but she longed for the will of God in her life no matter what the cost.

As Jesus touched her life, Marie drew closer to Him. She found a love like no other as prayer became an integral part of her life.

She worshiped from her soul and immersed herself in the Word. She discovered promises that she never knew before, as her experience with God grew deeper. Everything and everyone around her became second as she fell in love with Jesus. She felt peace and strength like never before.

Marie had to work much overtime to make ends meet, and the daily responsibilities of working and raising a child pressed her down. A couple from church volunteered to help take care of her daughter in order to ease her burden. They soon became like an adoptive family to Marie and her daughter. When she needed rest, they would take her daughter for a few days.

The Lord supplied Marie with a new home, and she transferred to another plant. She drew close to many families in the church, and they loved her as their own. She also had many friends at work who loved to joke and tease with her. Nevertheless, Marie longed for a companion. Her friends at work offered to help her find a husband, but she denied them as delicately as possible. She desired God's will in this matter. She desired a man who had the same convictions that she did and someone who truly loved God. She also needed someone who would love and care for her child as much as she did.

Marie became the good friend of a special lady at work named Sharon. They felt as if they were sisters and had known each other for years. They could share their concerns, problems, and even their deepest secrets. At work they would talk about their lives and solve any problems that came their way. Sharon sometimes even worked overtime with Marie to help her out. Soon others joined in their fellowship as they rejoiced with gospel songs and talked about the goodness of the Lord.

Sharon and others encouraged Marie to date those who would come around. She finally explained that she was looking for an Apostolic like herself.

One day as Marie was working and the others were on break, Sharon burst through the doors. She had a big smile on her face as she pulled a piece of paper from her pocket. "I got it! I got it!" Sharon exclaimed as she waved the paper in her hand. She began to tell Marie that she had found the perfect man for her, an Apostolic.

Trying not to look too interested, Marie gratefully took the paper and began to read it. Totally surprised, she tried to conceal her excitement as she realized that this person seemed to be everything she had been searching for. Laughingly, she told Sharon that she couldn't date someone she didn't even know. Sharon put his address in Marie's pocket and encouraged her to write him as she turned to leave. Marie pushed the thoughts from her mind; it had to be too good to be true.

That night as Marie was praying, her daughter wrapped her arms around her and asked, "Mama, will I ever have a daddy?" Marie encouraged her to pray about it as she tucked her daughter into bed. Turning off the lights, she headed to her own room. Tears began to burn in her eyes. She too was lonely, but as she crawled into bed the loneliness hit her especially hard. She hadn't realized till then just how lonely she was. She knew she had Jesus, but she wanted someone to share in her life.

As she lay there, she began to pray. Suddenly she remembered the paper in her jacket pocket. She was apprehensive because she didn't even know the man, but the Lord reminded her that, if nothing else, he too needed a friend.

She thought about it for a few weeks and finally decided to write. She decided not to tell anyone until she knew a little more herself. After several days of waiting, Marie's reply finally came. Nervously she ripped the letter open and began to read. Her heart filled with excitement. She found her dreams written in the letter.

Bubbling with happiness, Marie decided to keep the matter to herself until she knew more. Trying to question those around her without drawing suspicion, she found that others from her church had met the man. Eager to find out more, she continued to write him. She soon discovered that his name was Wayne. Just as God had said, he too was lonely and needed a friend. She was excited to find out that he also had a strong love for God.

Marie and Wayne loved to talk about God as they continued to write to one another. With each letter Wayne made her laugh more and more. She found herself falling in love even though she hadn't even met him yet. She did her best to deny the love she felt, because of the abusive scars still hidden deep in her life. But each letter began to strengthen their friendship as she learned that their convictions were much the same. Holding his letters in her hands, she shook her head in disbelief, still feeling that it was all too good to be true.

One day while traveling with her sister to see their father, Marie realized that they were to pass right through Wayne's hometown on the return trip. When she informed Wayne of their route, he pleaded for them to stop and have dinner with him so they could meet at last. Knowing she had to meet him sometime, she thought it might be easier with her sister along.

Arriving at the agreed destination, Marie

became nervous. With each passing car, the urge to drive away became stronger, but Marie's sister encouraged her to be patient.

Finally the moment arrived. A car pulled into the parking lot, the car Wayne had described over the phone. Marie stepped from her own car, struggling to maintain her composure. Looking up, she noticed a tall, slender man with blondish brown hair and blue eyes.

Grasping a beautiful red rose in his hands, he approached her. With trembling hands he handed her the rose, and with an uneven voice he said, "Hello. I'm Wayne. I'm so glad you decided to stop."

As they sat down to eat dinner, Marie breathed a sigh of relief. The hardest part was over. As the conversation began, the stiffness in the air began to clear, and the atmosphere began to relax. It seemed as if they had known each other for years. The laughter continued. As the time drew closer to leave, Marie felt sad. She had found a friend like no other, and he loved God as much as she did.

On the way home, Marie's sister excitedly

declared, "You two are meant for each other!" Marie tried desperately not to fall in love, but it was too late. Tears fell from her eyes. Wayne had stolen her heart with his rose and his laughter. Never before had a man treated her with such compassion.

Each time Marie and Wayne talked and met after that first meeting, their love flourished. Marie did her best to deny her love for Wayne but found it overwhelming her. She struggled to make the right choice in her life. Fear began to envelop her as her relationship with Wayne advanced toward marriage.

Marie called Wayne to announce her decision to end the relationship before it went any further. Trying his best to understand, Wayne sought to ease Marie's fears and pain.

Marie tried desperately to wipe Wayne from her thoughts as the day continued but found it impossible. How could he love someone like her? she wondered. She concluded that it was best for their relationship to end.

As Marie struggled with the pain, she heard a knock on the door. There she was greeted by an unfamiliar lady with a basket of flowers. An attached card said, "God can see us through anything. I love you! Wayne."

As she put the flowers down on the table she knew God was still in control. She also knew in her heart that she loved Wayne more than ever.

Each time they were apart, the separation seemed endless. She counted the days till the next visit or the next phone call. When the phone rang she knew it was Wayne. She was glad to hear his encouraging voice say everything was going to be okay. Wayne told her that he would always be there for her and would help her through anything if she would let him. As she cried, Wayne inspired her to smile with his laughter.

Marie and Wayne excitedly made plans to attend a summer camp meeting. The devil seemed to fight Marie with everything he had. Determined to make it, she and a friend finally arrived at the campground three hours late due to car trouble. When they entered the tabernacle, it was full of praise and worship like Marie had never witnessed before. She stood there in amazement, thinking, This is what heaven will be like!

Losing herself in the worship, she was quickly brought back to reality with a nudge from her friend, Julie. Teasingly Julie announced, "There is your future husband running down the aisle!" She looked up to see Wayne. At that moment a voice behind her said, "If you're looking for a husband, that's the best place to find one." With her eyes still focused on Wayne, she quickly agreed and walked on to find a seat.

Marie and Wayne both knew that worship could lead them into a special realm with God. Marie began to think of just how far God had brought her as she watched Wayne worship. There was no way she could love God as He loved her, but she decided to try her best.

That weekend was the greatest time Marie had ever had. She stayed with church friends of Wayne's, and they made her feel welcome. Marie and Wayne both realized that weekend what God had done for each other. The journey home was especially hard for Marie as she longed to be with Wayne. Loneliness hit her like a flood as she drove up in her driveway.

When she walked into her house, the phone was ringing, and she hurried to answer it. She was delighted to hear Wayne's voice on the other end, and the loneliness started to lift.

The next day Marie had to get back to work, for she had missed a few more days than she had planned, due to car trouble. Her coworkers questioned her again and again about where she had been. Finally she confided to Sharon, "It was the greatest time of my life. He's everything I ever dreamed of. The only bad part was when I had to leave."

Sharon knew she was in love and replied, "It's too late. He's stolen your heart. You're in love, and there is no turning back." Marie knew Sharon was right; there was no sense in denying it any longer.

As time went on, their relationship became stronger. One night as they talked on the phone, Wayne became unusually quiet. Marie, concerned that something was wrong, began to question him. "Are you okay, Wayne? Have I done something?"

Wayne replied nervously, "I've been thinking. I can't live without you any longer! I want you with me every minute of the day. I can't stand to be here without you. Marie . . . would you marry me?"

Marie had settled into the life that she had built for herself a long time before, thinking she would be alone for the rest of her life. But Wayne had made all the pain leave with his laughter, and his love was unconditional. He was what she had searched for and longed for in her dreams.

Choking back her tears, Marie knew that she too needed Wayne as he needed her. With apprehension in her voice she replied, "Yes, that would make me the happiest person in the world."

Wayne breathed a sigh of relief, excited to hear Marie's reply. The phone began to buzz with excitement as the two talked about their future together.

During the following months of planning,

Marie perceived that something was amiss.
Those around her had begun to whisper. As
her suspicions grew she began to question
them, "What is wrong with everyone?" Trying
to comfort Marie and assure her that everything was okay, they told her she was only having last-minute jitters.

One night as she returned home from
work, Marie noticed a friend's car in her driveway. When she walked into her house, she was
surprised to see all her friends standing
around. They had planned a party to show
their love. Tears filled her eyes. She hadn't
realized till then just how many lives she had
touched and how many had touched hers.
Marie realized how blessed she was and how
hard it would be to leave all her friends and
church family.

As time went on, pressure began to build
with each decision. Finally Wayne, realizing
what Marie was going through, decided to go
and pick her up. He had a trailer that she could
live in till their wedding. With each good-bye she
found it harder and harder to remain strong.

A friend from church named Sue asked to speak with Marie privately. Sue had been like a mother to her and had always taken good care of her. She was always full of encouraging words and was someone Marie respected greatly as a godly lady. Knowing that Marie had fears about the direction she had chosen in her life, Sue comforted her with encouraging words. "God will always be there. If you make a wrong decision, God will forgive you. Whatever life brings you, always keep God first. Look to God for any answers you need in your life."

As Marie hugged Sue, she knew she had to go. She felt sadness touch her as she waved her last good-byes, but she also felt happiness for the life that was just beginning.

The wedding bells finally rang, and Wayne and Marie were united as one. They dedicated their lives to God and spoke their vows of commitment. Tears fell from Marie's face as she looked into Wayne's eyes. Tranquillity filled her heart. Grasping his hands, she promised her love to him forever.

"Mr. and Mrs." rang in Marie's ears as the preacher introduced them to the congregation. Smiling with a joy-filled heart, she noticed all their loved ones who had come to share their happiness. As the celebration continued she realized just how blessed she was. Even though she still had fears, she knew God was there to see her through every situation.

Marie found pleasure in her work and in pleasing Wayne. They taught their children the happiness of living for God with many hours of fun and laughter. Together the family enriched their lives with each other.

Seven ~

A Plea for Help

Walking back into her house, Marie shook her head in disbelief as she drifted back to reality. She fell to her knees and began to cry out to God.

Marie wept bitterly. What had crashed down on top of her? She had gotten victory over her past. Why was it haunting her now? Tears burned in her eyes, exhaustion finally took over, and she faded off to sleep.

The morning light peered through the window and awoke Marie. Sitting up, she felt the tiredness from the night's events. Wiping her eyes, she noticed her children looking at her with concern. Not wanting to answer any questions, she hurried off to prepare their breakfast.

Marie realized that her husband and children were not her problem, so she struggled not to withdraw from them. Nevertheless, as her children reached out for affection, she often found herself avoiding them. Disheartened by her past, she allowed shame to imprison her emotions.

Something inside pleaded for Marie to reach for her family. But with each attempt, Marie only fell deeper into depression. She tried desperately to pray and to understand, but it seemed that God was nowhere to be found.

When she scolded her children, she heard herself using words that her stepfather had spoken to her. She knew this wasn't the biblical way to raise her children, and her reactions disturbed her.

Marie and Wayne had found a wonderful church that made them feel just like family. The church was an answer to prayer for both of them. The people loved each other with an unconditional love. The power of God was strong, and the services lifted them up each time they went. They longed for church time as it drew near. Not having God-fearing families, they experienced a new family life that they had never known. But now Marie needed a friend, and she found herself withdrawing instead of reaching for help. She knew people in the church would help but found it hard to ask.

She talked to Wayne about her fears, and he tried to encourage her as best he could. He told her the church was her help, and the people there would help her find answers from God. Wayne loved the church and its refuge, and so had Marie until now. She didn't want anyone to know just how weak she felt. She grew hard as she withdrew. She began to get angry with God as she searched in vain for answers.

Even at night Marie began to withdraw. She didn't want to be held, and tears burned in her eyes. Marie held her cries so as not to wake Wayne, as she tried to keep from losing her sanity. How could she allow this to happen? she thought. Not only had she ruined her life, but now she would ruin the life of her husband and children.

As Marie struggled with the dreams and images, she longed to escape. She understood the pain her abusive past would unfold if she reached for help. On the other hand, she could no longer continue to sit still while she watched her life slowly deteriorate. Feeling the pressures overwhelm her, she knew she would explode if she didn't ask for help.

When the church service started one night, Marie felt tears welling up in her eyes. Trying to keep her composure, she listened anxiously to the Word for direction. She went to the front when the altar call came. She wanted God's will in every situation in her life. She had found a wonderful life with her family and church and didn't want to leave, but she felt there was no other choice.

As she prayed she felt led to talk to her pastor's wife, Sister Ainsworth. Marie really didn't know her very well, but she had great confidence in her as a prayer warrior, for she had seen Sister Ainsworth intercede many times. She had the utmost respect for her, more than for anyone else. She was a godly lady who encouraged and loved others and who followed God's leading. Sister Ainsworth could help her find an answer if anyone could.

Standing up, Marie approached Sister Ainsworth and asked to speak with her in private. She trembled with fear, but she realized that she had to trust someone. Despite an urge to retreat, she nervously followed Sister Ainsworth into another room.

With a concerned look, Sister Ainsworth questioned, "Is something wrong?"

With tear-filled eyes Marie tried desperately to explain. "I just can't go on like this any longer. I'm tired and I can't press through. It seems as if I can't find God anywhere. The more I pray, the more distant I feel. I need to get away for a while to clear my mind."

Quickly Sister Ainsworth reassured Marie, "Running isn't going to help. You'd be surprised at the saints who have come to me over the last month or so. The devil knows his time is short, and he's opened up his arsenal. You just have to hang in there and keep praying."

"I'm just too tired to go on. I can't sleep at night because of dreams. I've become discouraged. I don't intend to backslide, but I need some time to myself." Marie groaned as she leaned against the wall.

Sister Ainsworth, concerned over the dreams, asked, "Dreams? What kind of dreams?"

Realizing she had said more than she had intended, Marie quickly tried to cover her mistake. "Oh . . . nothing. . . . I'll be fine. I just need a little rest."

Still concerned, Sister Ainsworth reassured Marie that she and her husband would bind together and pray for Marie. Before Marie left, Sister Ainsworth prayed with her, and she began to feel the pressure lift. Trying to avoid any further conversation, she quickly smiled as she thanked Sister Ainsworth.

At home that night, feeling confident because of her conversation with Sister Ainsworth, Marie knelt down to pray. She thanked the Lord for her church and pastor and slipped into bed reassured. God's peace overshadowed her. Drifting off to sleep, Marie cried tears of joy and knew things could only get better.

In the middle of the night, Marie was awakened by another terrorizing dream.

Trembling with fear and distress, she made her way into the living room and collapsed in her chair. Moaning with despair, Marie began to allow the abuse from her childhood to take control again. Visions began to flood her mind as she lost control of her thoughts.

Once again she relived the abuse. She saw herself running from home as she tried to escape. She ran faster and faster, ignoring the thorns as they ripped the skin on her legs and arms. She lost her footing, fell into a ditch, and cried with agonizing pain as rocks broke her fall. Seeing headlights in the distance, she muffled her cries and crawled deeper into the ditch. She shivered from the dampness of the grass and tried to catch her breath. With heart pounding, she resumed her flight. To elude traffic, Marie ran deeper into the woods. Finally, exhausted and confused, she collapsed to the ground.

Realizing that she had lost her way in the woods, Marie began to whimper uncontrollably. In pain, she began to pray that death would come. She had nowhere to turn, and she felt that there was no reason to live.

Marie soon fell asleep, only to be awakened by the morning light. Shivering from the dampness of her clothes, she pulled herself from the ground. Half frozen, her body trembled with pain. It was bloodstained from the night before. Each cut stung as the warmth began to fill her limbs. Dazed and confused, she began walking again, stumbling with each step. She had to find help.

As the morning light broke through the window, Marie struggled to fend off these thoughts and return to reality. Things seemed hopeless; she was still in the same predicament. Discouraged greatly, she began to weep, feeling that there was no end to her abuse. It was still controlling her life years later. At that moment, she realized that running only aggravated her problem; she needed to seek help.

The phone began to ring in the distance. Happy to leave her thoughts, Marie answered it quickly. Hearing Sister Ainsworth on the other end, Marie tried to sound encouraged.

Sister Ainsworth's first question soon brought silence, however. She inquired about the events from the night before and became disturbed when Marie didn't reply. Marie muffled her cries and couldn't answer. Trying to encourage her, Sister Ainsworth said, "I don't understand it all, but we will continue in our prayers."

As the conversation continued, Sister Ainsworth soon realized that Marie was hiding something. "If you ever want to talk, you can come to me," Sister Ainsworth offered, realizing that she was dealing with a case of abuse.

Marie wanted to divert the conversation from the truth. She thanked Sister Ainsworth and hung up the phone.

When Wayne came home, Marie informed him of her conversation with Sister Ainsworth. Wayne encouraged her to talk to Sister Ainsworth. Concerned over the dreams, he knew that she needed someone she could trust.

Marie was fearful of telling everything to Sister Ainsworth, but she was at her rope's end. She was standing at a crossroads.

Marie debated her options and finally realized that she had no other choice but to trust someone. Sister Ainsworth was a kind-hearted person and would be easy to talk with. While it would be hard to disclose the abuse to her, Marie knew it was slowly destroying her and she had nowhere else to turn.

Picking up the phone, Marie decided to call Sister Ainsworth and set up a time to talk before she lost her nerve. They made plans to meet the next day.

Marie began to regret her decision as soon as she hung up. What will she think of me? she wondered. Why did I ever say anything? She wanted to turn back, but she had already gone beyond the point of return.

Anger began to build up for allowing herself to trust again. The more she thought about it, the angrier she became at herself. How could I be so foolish as to say anything? Why didn't I just keep my mouth shut?

Marie argued with herself as she drove towards the church for the appointment. Feeling herself lose control, she fought back tears. "Lord, I need Your help," she pleaded. "Please give me the strength. Don't let me run this time."

Eight ✍

Reaching Out

$\mathcal{S}$itting down in the office, Marie tried not to panic. Sister Ainsworth began the discussion with typical conversation, and Marie began to feel more at ease as she spoke. She tried to disguise her fear and add to the conversation as much as possible.

Sister Ainsworth soon realized that Marie was trying to stall. She said, "However you want to start is fine with me."

Marie froze. What can I say? she thought. What do I say? How do I say it? Why did Sister Ainsworth have to change the conversation? Taking a deep breath, she tried to speak. She tried to laugh as she covered her true feelings.

She diverted the conversation away from the abuse, recalling many things in her life that she didn't mind talking about.

Marie's stepfather had been a harsh man, especially when it came to discipline within the family. If the children dared to cross him or disobey him, they were punished severely. They lived like slaves. Their day consisted of rigorous work, and they worked from early morning till late hours of the night.

When they weren't working, they tried to stay away from their stepfather. They knew better than to disturb him, because if they did, he would find another a job or punishment would come. Sometimes when one child mis-behaved he would punish all of them to make sure it wouldn't happen again. If he called a child to his side, the child had better not hesi-tate, for doing so brought a punishment no one could ever forget.

Her stepfather could send chills of fear with just a look. The townspeople who knew him either hated him or treated him with respect. No one dared to step out of line with him. Many became terrorized just by his presence.

Marie often wondered what his childhood had been like, because he seldom showed emotion. From time to time he would surprise them, but most of the time he held his solemn face.

As alcohol became more prevalent in the home, so did the arguments between Marie's mother and stepfather. They began to produce their own alcohol at home. They would bottle and cap it themselves, and sometimes they would help themselves to a drink or two while they bottled it.

One day, as the fighting increased, Marie exploded with anger. "Stop it, please!" Marie pleaded. "No more fighting. Just shut up." Then she pushed her stepfather away from her mother.

Marie froze in her tracks. What had she done?

Immediately the blow of his fists came, and Marie was thrown against the wall. "You're next!" her stepfather announced as he turned to finish the fight with her mother.

Marie quietly slid out the back door. Running down the road, she ran until she reached the church. There was a cemetery beside it that contained a statue of Jesus. Kneeling down beside it, Marie prepared herself for the punishment she was to endure.

As she heard the echoes of an approaching motorcycle, Marie stood to her feet and shook with terror. She knew her stepfather was coming to retrieve her. To her surprise, he merely stared at her and then he turned around and headed home. The motorcycle gained speed, and Marie knew that if he didn't slow down he'd never make the hill. As he topped the hill, he raised his hands into the air.

Just as he went out of sight, Marie heard a destructive crash. She hurdled the fence as she ran for the house. Blood was everywhere. His helmet, which lay in the middle of the road, was completely crushed.

Marie ran into the house. She gasped for air and stood frozen in her tracks. There sat her stepfather in his chair solemnly. His collarbone stuck out from his shoulder. His body looked as if an animal had shredded his skin.

With anger in his voice, her stepfather refused to be taken to the hospital. She couldn't believe her eyes, for he showed no emotion from the pain. What kind of person could sit there without even a whimper? She realized then that he was different from any person she had ever known. He was a hard, cold man, and she wondered what had made him that way.

Her mom wanted to call an ambulance, but her stepfather threatened to kill her if she dared. Marie's older brother ran out the door and informed the neighbors of the crash. They immediately called for an ambulance, ignoring the threats. They informed her stepdad that he was going to the hospital. He was in no shape to resist; the ambulance soon carried him off.

Even though Marie felt a certain sense of freedom, she still prayed that he would live. As much as she resented him, she didn't wish anyone to die. She even visited him when given the opportunity a few weeks later and felt pity as she walked from the room. No matter how badly he had hurt her, she couldn't wish any harm to him.

As Marie recounted this story, Sister Ainsworth realized that she was stalling again. "Let's discuss the dreams," she requested.

Stunned, Marie argued, "Why is it so important to discuss the dreams?"

"You have to talk about them and let the problem out. If you don't, it will eat at you until it destroys you."

Marie choked as she tried to speak. Each time she tried to talk about the abuse, she found herself pushing back anger. When she closed her eyes, the images became real and the abuse began. Pain and guilt still lurked within.

In one tragic night Marie's life was devastated by her abusive stepfather. That night Marie's life became a nightmare. She had always been an energetic and fun-loving child who laughed often. But after that night she began to withdraw as filth and ugliness overpowered her. Believing she was partially responsible, Marie felt humiliated. Why had this hap-

happened? What had she done? Marie's self-respect deteriorated as the abuse continued.

These memories flooded her thoughts as she tried to confide in Sister Ainsworth. Silence prevailed. Feeling as if the last thread of life had begun to unravel, she starting convulsing with rage. Her blood pressure began to rise as she struggled to contain the pain.

Sister Ainsworth realized that something was wrong and delicately tried to comfort and ease Marie. Although Marie desperately wanted help, pain overwhelmed her. She tried repeatedly to speak. Feeling the walls begin to close in, she quickly burst from the office with the excuse of needing air. She staggered into the restroom and rinsed her face with cool water in hopes of easing her anguish.

By this time, her face was flushed red. Fighting back her tears, she prayed that God would help her. Her body quivered uncontrollably. She began to weep but quickly pulled herself together lest Sister Ainsworth hear her. Wanting to end the discussion, she decided to return to the office.

In humiliation, she apologized to Sister Ainsworth as she slipped back into her seat. Sister Ainsworth compassionately urged Marie, "Take it slow."

Marie covered her face in shame, regretting her decision to come. She tried earnestly to change the subject, but Sister Ainsworth insisted that she return to the abuse.

"Don't you understand?" Marie pleaded "It's harder than you could ever imagine. I can't . . . I just can't."

Sister Ainsworth realized that this might be her only opportunity to help Marie, so she repeatedly asked Marie to return to the previous conversation.

Feeling betrayed Marie asked, "Why do you keep insisting that I talk?"

Sister Ainsworth replied, "Your anger and problems are wrapped around one root, and they need to be dug up."

Sister Ainsworth's digging was more persistent than Marie expected. Frightened that Sister Ainsworth would uncover her secrets, Marie began to shake. Sweat poured from her forehead.

Marie's intention had been just to reveal a little bit, and then she expected everything to get better. But Sister Ainsworth wanted to dig deeper. Each time Marie tried to veer a different direction, Sister Ainsworth always led her back to the beginning. Marie began to feel as if Sister Ainsworth didn't understand. Completely frustrated, she laughed to disguise her true feelings and disregarded the anger that was building up. She felt deep in her heart that no one could ever fully understand without actually being there all those years.

Realizing the time of day, Marie felt relief. She began to use the time as an excuse to leave. Sister Ainsworth urged Marie to finish so she could begin to heal, but in the face of Marie's persistence in leaving, Sister Ainsworth finally informed her that she was free to leave whenever she wanted.

Marie jumped at the chance to escape. Without thinking, she stood and walked from the office. She paused outside the door and fought for courage to turn around, but then she walked on. She knew she had disappointed Sister Ainsworth.

As she walked to her vehicle, sadness flooded her mind. She felt that her secret was wide open as a book, and everyone could read it, even though she had not had the courage to admit the abuse. She found it almost impossible to smile and cover up the inner secrets she had protected for so many years. She could no longer perform her charades. She felt more alone than ever, for she couldn't face talking to Sister Ainsworth again. Her fears became reality: now she had no one to turn to.

Nine 🖎

Humility's Grip

Marie was grateful that her evening schedule held dinner plans for her and Wayne. It would allow her thoughts to be temporarily out of service, as she was anxious to forget the day's events.

She was thankful when the evening finally came to an end. As Marie and Wayne drove toward home, they talked about the day's events. Wayne became irritated with Marie as she explained that she couldn't talk. He tried to convince her that she needed to apologize to Sister Ainsworth, because she was only trying to help.

Wayne felt that Marie's conversation with Sister Ainsworth wasn't what it should have been. He told her that she should have taken it more seriously.

Extremely discouraged, Marie pushed the conversation out of her head. As Wayne and Marie crawled into bed, Marie found it difficult to sleep. So many issues were left unsettled.

Marie's dreams kept her tossing all night. Nightmares haunted her again.

As the days passed, God put her in a position where she couldn't keep herself busy any longer. She began to dwell upon her life and how she had ruined it.

Too humiliated to attend church, Marie found herself making excuses to stay home. Wayne, realizing what she was doing, insisted that she attend again.

When Sister Ainsworth walked into church, Marie quickly darted in the other direction. She couldn't even bear to look at her, let alone have a discussion with her. Humiliated because she had said too much, she quickly made her way to Wayne's side. Hoping silently that Sister Ainsworth wouldn't come by, Marie breathed a sigh of relief when the service started. Her nerves began to settle as the preaching began. She found herself engrossed in the word, and she began to feel better as the word touched her heart.

At the altar call, Marie knelt at her seat to pray. She felt her anxiety begin to lift as God touched her. Feeling extremely guilty for dodging Sister Ainsworth, Marie realized that she was only trying to help. As she rose from her seat, she noticed Sister Ainsworth looking at her. When their eyes met, Marie quickly smiled to hide her embarrassment.

On the way home, she knew she needed to sort things out before they destroyed everything she loved. She puzzled over her thoughts as she fought with the adversary. What had she hoped to happen when she talked to Sister Ainsworth? Had she expected to gain a friend, or did she want someone to feel sorry for her? She didn't know what she wanted, but she did know that she needed to get control of herself. She had been completely satisfied with her life, and then everything had changed. Now she was frozen in her thoughts, trying to decide her next step.

As Marie began her next day, she knew she

could take no more. She picked up the phone to call Sister Ainsworth. Not really knowing what to say, she apologized for her actions during their conversation. Sister Ainsworth quickly explained to Marie that she hadn't done anything wrong. She understood Marie's struggle. Marie apologized for dodging her the night before, but Sister Ainsworth understood that too.

As they talked, Marie felt better with each word. She hadn't realized till then how much compassion Sister Ainsworth really had. She couldn't understand how Sister Ainsworth could be so nice after she had treated her so badly. Marie explained that she didn't want Sister Ainsworth to feel sorry for her but she just needed a friend to talk to. Sister Ainsworth agreed and told Marie she'd always be there if Marie wanted to talk again.

Although she knew it would be difficult to talk, Marie quickly made arrangements for another conversation. Down deep, Marie longed for a closer walk with God. She knew she needed God more than ever before in her life. In all the darkness, she felt a hunger growing inside. She wanted to give her life completely to God, and she wanted to become what He wanted her to be. In order to accomplish that, she would have to let God purge her.

As she hung up with Sister Ainsworth, she remembered a tape of an evangelist that might help. She couldn't find that tape, but she found a different message by the same evangelist and began to listen to it. As he spoke, she couldn't believe what she was hearing. She had completely forgotten what was on that tape. He was saying, "Not only does God want to deliver you, but He wants to heal you. God wants to complete the work He has started."

Marie thought back to the beginning of her life for Jesus. The words of her first pastor echoed in her ears: "Therefore if any man be in Christ, he is a new creature: old things are passed away; behold all things are become new" (II Corinthians 5:17). Marie had rejoiced at the time, thinking her past was completely healed when she was born again. But now she realized that Jesus had simply begun the complete healing process when she was born again. If He had put her through the complete process at once, she would not have been able to handle it. She would have died during the surgery. She had not been prepped (prepared), but now her time had come. It was time to remove the malignant cells of the adversary within.

As she listened to the tape, Marie's understanding increased. The man of God compared emotional and spiritual wounds to a pimple or a boil. Initially, there is a sore spot that grows worse and worse because something inside needs to come out. As time continues, pressure begins to build. It irritates everything around it. A few days later the lump appears on the surface. If the infection is allowed to come out, healing will begin, but if not, the pain will increase.

Just as God has a healing process for the body, He also has a healing process for the spirit. As a spiritual infection builds, it has to work itself out. If it doesn't, the whole spirit can become infected. In order to heal, we must allow the Holy Spirit to purify us from all spiritual filth.

Marie realized what needed to happen. As painful as it would be, everything had to come out.

Ten 🖝

Tearing Down Strongholds

In a conversation with Sister Ainsworth again, Marie struggled to talk. Sister Ainsworth pleaded with Marie just to begin and then to continue.

Marie's pain began to surface. She fought back tears as scenes began to flash through her mind. Marie covered her eyes with clenched fists. As Marie began to relive her nightmares, Sister Ainsworth pleaded for her to face them.

The pressure was great, and anger flooded her. Unable to control her emotions, Marie let out an agonizing cry. As her cries began to ring out boisterously, she felt the coldness of her escape. She remembered the concrete tube as her security; now it haunted her mind as she struggled to escape it. Her body trembled uncontrollably, and she dropped her face into her hands. The abuse continued to pour out, and as her cries rang throughout the room. Marie's agony only increased. She couldn't believe how much it still hurt. The anguish was as real as if she were still in the abusive situation. As she buried her face deeper in her hands, the humiliation and condemnation kept her from reaching out.

Remembering as a child how she longed for her mother to understand, she began to weep bitterly. Abused and broken, she just wanted someone to understand the pain. But the shackles of worthlessness and guilt kept Marie silent. While the battle raged within her mind, Marie fought to admit that she had been abused. Fighting to speak it, she found herself denying the truth. Completely exasperated, Marie shook her head to alert Sister Ainsworth that she wasn't going to continue.

"It's not going to be easy no matter how

you go about it." Sister Ainsworth responded. "But the longer you wait, the stronger it grows. You must allow the abuse to come out, so you can begin to heal. Even after you face it, I'll still be here to talk. Just because you tell me doesn't mean I won't be here."

Angered by her comment, Marie burst with frustration. She choked on her thoughts: Does she think I'm keeping my silence because I want her attention? She felt the hard blow of betrayal smack her right in the face. Disgraced by her thoughts, she stared at the floor, trying to push them from her mind as her heart broke. Doesn't anyone understand? Can she not see the pain it causes to talk about it? Marie just didn't know if she had the strength to go through it again.

The pain . . . the suffering . . . the hurt . . . and now the loneliness . . . Was Sister Ainsworth prepared for the journey?

Stone-faced with disgust, Marie forced herself to speak. What did she have to lose? She felt as if Sister Ainsworth just couldn't understand, but she had no choice now. She had to tell her story.

Feeling completely abandoned, Marie denied the pain that ripped through her heart. Ignoring the agonizing bitterness and determined not to look fragile, she held her solid exterior as she relived her nightmares. Marie shook her head in astonishment when she realized she was revealing her hidden thoughts. It was hard to tear the veil of secrecy and shame. At the verge of breaking, Marie pleaded with Sister Ainsworth to stop the conversation.

Realizing that Marie had to finish, Sister Ainsworth began to ask questions to further the conversation. "Marie, don't hold it back. Let it all come out. What happened next?"

Marie struggled to talk as she continued to recall her past. The brutal scenes flashed through her mind, though she fought to restrain them. Her tormented past instantly became her future, and anguish surfaced with each word she spoke. Marie's body began to shake with violent sobs.

Marie clasped her hands together, and her knuckles whitened under the pressure of the grip. The bitterness continued to pour out until she became exhausted. Ultimately silence prevailed.

Sister Ainsworth knew that Marie needed to conquer the internal battle and give everything to God. She had to completely surrender her memories and pain. "Is that all?" Sister Ainsworth asked as she glanced at Marie.

Exhausted from the anger, Marie struggled with her emotions. Have I said enough? Should I confide completely in her? Can I admit my guilt? Can I admit the abuse? How can I live with myself until I can? Enough, I can't take any more.

Unable to continue, Marie assured Sister Ainsworth that she was finished. "That's it." Marie sat in silence, feeling as if her body had been drained. Pressed down by guilt, her arms were heavy and her head hung in shame. She wanted to cry, but she held her peace.

Sister Ainsworth tried to comfort Marie and ease her pain. She reassured Marie that she was not to blame. "You were only an innocent child! You did not deserve what happened.

Please believe me, it's not your fault."

Marie refused to be comforted, feeling as if Sister Ainsworth just couldn't understand. She had blocked many of the memories from her thoughts, but what she did recall greatly disturbed her. Many nights she had pretended to be asleep in hopes of avoiding her stepfather. But I never fought back, she told herself. How could anyone understand? It was all my fault, and I'll never believe differently! These thoughts flooded Marie as she concealed the tears. She had vowed never to become feeble again, never again to let anyone take advantage of her.

The wall that Marie had built around herself had been completely destroyed, and its comfort was now erased. Even though it had kept her captive, it had also sheltered her from hurt. Now she had no defense. She was angry with Sister Ainsworth, holding her responsible for the destruction of the wall. The loneliness still lay within; she had nowhere to run.

Sister Ainsworth sensed the feeling of despair and said, "We need to leave this room!

We don't have to leave the church, but we need to go to another room." Sister Ainsworth hurried Marie from the room, but to reassure Marie that she wasn't trying to rush her off, she asked, "Do you want to talk some more? If not, we can pray or even have lunch."

Marie wanted to cry out, "Why did my mother abandon me when I protected her? Why would no one hear my cries? Why do I still feel bad when I have opened up? Will the hurt ever stop?" But feeling she had caused enough inconvenience, she held her questions. Apologizing, Marie headed for the door to leave.

Sister Ainsworth, still concerned, asked again, "You're sure you don't want to pray? How about lunch?"

Guilt stricken and completely disheartened, Marie just wanted to retreat and seek cover as the humiliation began to grow. "Thanks for your help," she replied. "I think it's time to go. I appreciate all you have done."

Marie was astonished that she had allowed the wall to fall. She felt completely defenseless. How could she have allowed Sister Ainsworth to crush her wall? she wondered. She had never allowed anyone close to it before. For many years she had maintained her fortress, but now she had allowed it to fall. Now she could no longer hide behind the wall as a defense.

Sister Ainsworth felt helpless. She knew Marie was hurting, but she also understood that she had walked with her as far as she could. Marie would have to finish the journey alone. There were decisions in Marie's life that only she could make. Sister Ainsworth could only pray and hope that Marie would make the right decisions.

As Marie drove off, she found it impossible to look back. She wished that she could go back in time and erase all she had said. She began to weep, and soon she had to pull off the road. Her cries echoed through the car as she could no longer hold them back. In anguish, Marie gripped the steering wheel, thinking that the only thing she had done was to hurt Sister Ainsworth and ruin their friendship. How can

Sister Ainsworth respect me, knowing what she knows? she thought. How can I ever live with someone knowing? Will I feel like this forever?

That night, Marie was easily agitated. When the phone rang, she was surprised to hear her stepfather on the other end. Terrorized by his voice, she trembled as she talked. Wayne held her hand, trying to comfort her. Her stepfather had only called to get information on her brother, but she felt as if he knew she had talked and was letting her know.

Marie put the children to bed earlier than usual, despite their complaints. She needed time alone to sort through the day's events. Slipping out the back door, she sought solitude in the night air. She sat down by an old tree and began to pray.

"Lord, please take this confusion from me. Allow Your peace to overshadow me. Whatever this is that I don't understand, please make it go away. I need Your joy back in my life. I want true happiness. Use me, Lord. Whatever good can come of this, Lord, please show me. Without You I can't go on. Let my light shine for Your glory and not my own. Take my horrible life and turn it into something You can use. Take my brokenness and remake it into Your vessel. Give me the strength to do Your will. Not my will, but Your will, be done."

She finished her prayer and hurried back into the house before she was missed. After getting ready for bed, Marie informed Wayne that she was tired and felt like going to sleep. As they crawled into bed, Marie pulled away from Wayne. She needed some space to clear her mind. But each time she closed her eyes, the images of the abuse returned. She tossed and turned as she tried to fall asleep.

Finally, Marie fell into a deep sleep. As she slept her dreams became reality. She began to plead with her stepfather, "Please, no more. I didn't tell anyone. Please don't hit me again." As his laughter rang out, she pleaded for help.

The next thing Marie knew, her husband was standing beside their bed shaking her vigorously. He wiped her face with a cool towel and pleaded with her to wake up. She noticed fear in his eyes. She assured him that she was awake but then began to sob uncontrollably. Wayne held her until she drifted back to sleep.

As the days passed, Marie immersed herself in the Bible and in preaching tapes. One day Marie felt the touch of the Lord as she read James 5:16: "Confess your faults one to another, that ye may be healed. The effectual fervent prayer of a righteous man availeth much."

Marie thought about the verse of Scripture as she read it again. "Maybe Sister Ainsworth was right after all. Maybe it was what I needed," Marie spoke to herself. Then she shook her head. "No, I don't understand how it helped. I just can't see it right now." Examining the passage of Scripture closer, she realized the need of prayer more than ever. She already prayed every day, but now she felt the Lord drawing her into a deeper realm. She fell to her knees and began to pray. She felt God's touch, and tears flowed from her eyes.

Understanding a little more, she began to fast more. As her prayer life grew, she felt the adversary war against her. Life seemed to demand more from her than ever. But this time she knew she had the Lord and His promises to lean on.

Eleven ✍

Picking up the Pieces

As Marie sat in the pew waiting for church to start, she reached for her Bible. She opened it to Romans 8 and began to read. The Lord began to speak to her.

Marie felt condemnation in her heart and questioned it. She soon realized that her flesh was dying, but her spirit was becoming stronger. She reached Romans 8:28: "And we know that all things work together for good to them that love God, to them who are the called according to his purpose." Never before had Marie thought that God might have a purpose for her. She had always felt unworthy.

Choking back her tears, she recalled the

night that she prayed for God's highest will in her life. Somewhere along the way she had forgotten that request. She had never lost the desire; now it was stronger than ever. God could take all her anger and pain and make something good of it.

Marie awakened to reality when she heard the voice of her pastor. Turning to Ezekiel 37, Brother Ainsworth began to read about the valley of dry bones. Listening to the reading of the Word, Marie felt encouraged. She knew that Brother Ainsworth had a word from the Lord.

She remembered her prayer of a few nights earlier: "Lord, why do I feel this way? My life has been shattered, and I feel so useless. No matter what I do, I can't seem to reach You. Why do I feel so cold and indifferent? What good can come of this?"

As Brother Ainsworth continued, Marie began to relate his words to her own life. She too felt as if hope was lost and her situation was impossible. She felt like a victim of captivity with the pain and scars of battle. Her life had become like a pile of dry bones. The battles in her life had seemingly shattered any hope for her to become anything great in God. But now, she realized, through God anything was possible.

Brother Ainsworth then began to relate a story that captured Marie's attention. An accomplished musician went to a distinguished instrument maker. The musician had much money and wanted a violin of the very best quality. When the musician tried the first instrument, he became enraged. Grabbing the violin by the neck, he smashed it into the floor and walked out the door.

A few months later the maker asked the musician to return to try another violin. Picking it up, the violinist drew the bow across the strings. As the music rang out, the crowds began to come. Song after song brought a smile to the musician's face. Turning to the maker, the musician asked, "Where did you come up with this one?"

The maker told him it was the one he had shattered on the floor. "After you left I picked up the pieces and glued them back together. I came to the realization that broken things, when put back together, make music like nothing else."

Brother Ainsworth then made the application. The touch of the Master's hand can complete anything. The breath of God's Spirit can put new life and a new anointing on any life, even on dried bones.

Tears began to stream down Marie's face as she saw the broken pieces of her life. She fell to her knees at the altar. Crying out to God, she felt the Master's hand as it once again touched her life. As she continued to pray, the pain began to surface. The hurt began to pour out. There was no wall to hold it back as it flowed out like a river.

Marie pleaded for God to pick up the shattered pieces of her life and make use of them. She became exhausted, but she wiped the sweat from her brow and pressed on, because she knew God was doing a work. She felt the Lord begin to restore things in her life that had been destroyed. She lifted her hands to praise the Lord, and the Lord began to bless her. Her spirit soared as the Master put her shattered pieces back together.

When Marie rose up from the altar, she was met with a hug from a woman in the church, Sister Sarah. Through that simple hug Marie felt an unconditional love that she had never felt before. It made everything seem all right. Marie knew she was no longer walking alone.

A few services later, Marie listened as a visiting preacher testified. Her heart lifted when he read Galatians 5:1: "Stand fast therefore in the liberty wherewith Christ hath made us free, and be not entangled again with the yoke of bondage." Marie began to think about the liberty that Christ had given her. Her yoke of bondage had been shattered. Praying at the altar that night, she thanked the Lord for giving her strength to endure the bondage she had been in. She finally realized that God had never left her; it was His strength that had enabled her to endure.

Twelve 🖎

The Journey of Healing

few weeks later, Marie became excited as she prepared to attend a women's conference. The theme was "Anointed for the Harvest." Marie needed a fresh anointing even though she had been blessed greatly by God. Marie began to fast and pray for the conference. Longing for a closer walk with God, she knew that if she could only make the conference, her life would be changed forever.

As she entered the tabernacle for the first session of the conference, Marie felt a deep urgency in her spirit. Anointed music filled the air, worship rang out, and the Spirit of the Lord began to fall.

Marie prayed like the psalmist David: "O God, thou art my God; early will I seek thee: my soul thirsteth for thee, my flesh longeth for thee in a dry and thirsty land, where no water is: to see thy power and thy glory, so as I have seen thee in the sanctuary" (Psalm 63:1-2).

When the opening speaker greeted and welcomed all the ladies, Marie knew that God had heard her prayers. His words moved within her heart, for they were an answer to her prayers: "God is here to heal all that has been devastated by the master of deceit. God has come to mend the broken-hearted and to refresh each lady with a new anointing."

Lord, can I be a vessel for Your use? Can You use someone like me? Marie thought as she recalled the dreams that had plagued her life over the previous months.

Marie's hardened surface began to break. Tears began to fall as memories flashed through her mind. Trying to conceal her painful recollections from those around her, she quickly lowered her head.

The Lord spoke to Marie's heart: "The

choice is yours. Will you reach for My nail-scarred hands? I am here to restore your joy and peace. Reach out and give everything to Me."

Feeling unworthy, Marie asked, "Why do I feel so terrible? What has happened to my joy? Why has my life been turned upside down?"

Marie soaked up the anointed preaching like a sponge. The Lord spoke to her heart through each word. She felt life begin to flow through her hardened heart.

The service ended, to Marie's dismay. There was a break for dinner.

That night in the conference, it was standing room only. The power of the Holy Ghost hovered over the room. There was an air of expectancy and excitement. Looking around, Marie realized that many other women were searching for hope and answers.

As the music began and the praise began to ring out, Marie felt the battle begin to rage inside her. Struggling to break the bonds of captivity, she lifted her hands and cried out, "Lord, I can't handle this any longer. Please help me give it to You."

Anguish pierced her heart, and she began to sob uncontrollably. Pain overwhelmed her, and as she had done so many times, she tried to suppress it. Desperately she called on the name of the Lord, asking God to make her heart tender with His love.

Irritated with herself, Marie slowly eased back down into her seat. She felt the bitter tears of defeat. As her mind began to drift off, she recalled the words of David: "Preserve me, O God: for in thee do I put my trust" (Psalm 16:1).

"Lord, have I completely trusted You?" Marie questioned.

Feeling the tug of the Spirit, Marie reached for her Bible. Flipping through the pages, Marie noticed a verse of Scripture she had highlighted sometime before: "There hath no temptation taken you but such as is common to man: but God is faithful, who will not suffer you to be tempted above that ye are able; but will with the temptation also make a way to escape, that ye may be able to bear it" (I Corinthians 10:13). Without a doubt, God had heard her cry.

Turning to another passage that the Lord placed in her mind, Marie read, "Therefore my heart is glad, and my glory rejoiceth: my flesh also shall rest in hope" (Psalm 16:9). She had a spark of hope again. She read on: "Thou wilt shew me the path of life: in thy presence is fulness of joy; at thy right hand there are pleasures for evermore" (Psalm 16:11). This was the path of her life, but now she could completely understand the fullness of joy within her life.

Marie listened closely as the anointed speakers spoke. The Word of the Lord began to soothe the rage she felt within. She continued to find answers to questions she had asked of God in the previous months. Unable to control her tears, she felt them fall from her cheeks.

The final speaker asked the women to stand as she closed her thoughts. "You don't have to leave with the load you carried in. You can leave your burdens and heartaches with the Lord. If you'd only step out into the aisle, the Lord will meet you there. He can heal all that has been shattered and broken in each life. You can have the true anointing that God intended for your life."

The aisles began to fill. Feeling the tug of the Holy Spirit, Marie stepped into the aisle, acknowledging that she too needed to leave her burdens behind. She struggled to release her tormenting past, with its condemnation, pain, bitterness, and loneliness.

"Do you believe I can?" the Lord spoke to her. "Do you believe?"

Crying out for strength to overcome, Marie felt the arm of a sister wrap around her. She knew then that the Lord was there to heal, and she felt the strength of His anointing.

The painful memories flooded her mind, and she dropped her head into her hands. The anguish was as real as ever. Violent sobs poured from her body. A voice from within spoke to her: "Now is the time to heal. Allow the strongholds that have bound you to be released. Turn loose. Allow your bondage to be broken. Set yourself free from guilt and condemnation."

Marie's knees began to buckle. "Lord, I don't deserve Your mercy," she groaned in despair as she collapsed to the floor.

The flashback of her tormenting dreams haunted her. Sobbing aloud, she found it impossible to muffle her cries. She pressed her face to the floor and decided that she could not push back the pain any longer. As she let it pour out, the Lord spoke to her soul: "Forgive. Forgive those who have failed you . . . those who have abused you . . . and those who turned away."

As the faces of her abusers flashed through Marie's mind, compassion and forgiveness touched her heart.

The resentment Marie had against her mother began to go away. The love of the Lord healed her of the loneliness that she had suffered over the years because of the lack of motherly love. After many years of bitterness, her love for her mother was being restored.

"Lord, please save my mother. Show her Your love as You have shown it to me. Let her feel the love I feel. Allow the bondage of guilt to be healed." Marie wept as she recalled her mother's tear-stained face.

The tears that fell from Marie's face now became sorrow for all who had abused her. Tenderness filled her heart as she thought of the life they now lived in shame. "Please, Lord, give them peace. Show them mercy as You have showed it to me this day. They too need the love of God in their lives."

Forgiveness filled Marie's heart. The gaping wounds began to heal with the touch of the Lord. Healing filled her spirit as she communed with the Lord. Realizing that she had suffered long enough, she began to release the burdens that had held her captive for so long. As the chains of bondage broke, her spirit lifted and the pain faded. Marie felt the Lord wrap His arms around her, and she knew she would never be alone again.

Basking in the presence of the Lord, Marie shouted praise to God for the victory. She rose to her feet and began to smile with the joy of the Lord. "Thank You, Lord," she prayed. "Now I can be who I really am."

As Marie walked back to her seat, she saw Sister Ainsworth's smiling face. Immediately, she began to understand the significance of her journey. God had put Sister Ainsworth and many others in her life to help her, but somewhere along the way she had lost her sight. Marie had allowed the adversary to deceive her into believing it was her battle alone and no one really understood. She had allowed the adversary to use her defense to imprison her.

But now she rejoiced in the goodness of the Lord, for she once again had a vision. God had always been there, willing and waiting with outstretched hands, wanting Marie to trust in Him completely. "Will you now allow My touch to do its work, allow My love to guide your heart?" He asked. "Reach out and allow the healing to begin."

"Yes, Lord," Marie answered. "Here I am!"

As her journey of healing approached a conclusion, Marie beheld a new vision. The end of the path was in sight, but now another journey lay ahead. With each journey's end, she would reach a deeper love and a closer walk with the Lord. The journey had been extremely rugged, and Marie didn't want to look back. As she looked to her future, however, she knew that God would be there to guide and protect her.

For God had shown her, the journey itself had been the key to her healing!

Just as Marie had taken a journey of healing, many other struggles that she could not imagine lay ahead. But it was the struggle itself that helped her build the will of God within her life. The pain was the hardest for Marie to conquer, because it lay within. She had forgiven all who had hurt her, except for the most important one—herself. The biggest battle she had fought was against the anger and guilt she had carried for so many years. She had believed that forgiveness was for everyone, except for the one who really needed it— Marie.

Although Marie had wanted instant healing, she found that healing came during the journey. It took Moses forty years to learn humility and leadership skills in a sheep field of Midian. Similarly, some wounds take years to develop and years to reveal themselves, and as a result it takes time for them to heal. God knows and understands our limitations; He knows what is best for us and when to bring it to pass. "To every thing there is a season, and a time to every purpose under the heaven," including "a time to heal" (Ecclesiastes 3:1, 3).

As Marie learned, when we find ourselves in a battle for spiritual healing, let us remember Ephesians 6:11: "Put on the whole armour of God, that you may be able to stand." God is able to help us stand and be victorious!

About the Author

Yvonne, a mother of four, currently lives in Malvern, Arkansas, with her husband, Timothy. She attends Apostolic Faith Tabernacle in Pearcy, Arkansas, where she teaches the Beginners Sunday school class. Yvonne is also involved in the church's orchestra and children's church. She has traveled worldwide: to New York City to play at Carnegie Hall, to Washington to perform for the president, and on a tour of Europe with her trumpet. Yvonne has recently joined her husband as a clown in hopes of starting a ministry for children.

For any questions or comments about the book, contact the author at:

Yvonne Rimmer
Rt 2, Box 150
Malvern, AR 72104

Telephone: 501-332-3049
E-mail: zipper@cswnet.com